100 Pics That Pr[...]

Is there any evidence that [...] [...], as so many myths and legends claim? Well, I'm going to share with you **101 pics and 101** that seem to suggest just that. The following list of pictures represents **circumstantial evidence at best**, that giants once walked the earth, and I invite you to approach them as a skeptic. However, as you examine each picture, ask yourself the following questions:

- Did all of these cultures invent the same myths and legends by coincidence?
- Is it possible that there is any truth to the legends of giants all around the world?
- Is it possible that evidence of giants in our past is being covered up by The Smithsonian, as many, including Steve Quayle (True Legends) have claimed?

More information about giants can be found on Steve Quayle's site Genesis 6 Giants.

1. The Old Testament Speaks of Giants Before and After The Flood

"There were giants in the earth in those days; and also after that, when the sons of God came in unto the daughters of men, and they bare *children* to them, the same *became* mighty men which *were* of old, men of renown." – Genesis 6:4

100 Pics That Prove Nephilim Giants Existed

If you want to learn more about nephilim giants in the Bible, then check out my book, As The Days of Noah Were: The Sons of God and The Coming Apocalypse.

2. Moses and Joshua Encountered Giants In The Promised Land

"And there we saw the giants, the sons of Anak, *which come* of the giants: and we were in our own sight as grasshoppers, and so we were in their sight." – Numbers 13:33

3. Rumor Has It That Giants Are Buried In Mounds Across America

"The eyes of that species of extinct Giant, whose bones fill the Mounds of America, have gazed on Niagara, as ours do now." – Abraham Lincoln, 1848

100 Pics That Prove Nephilim Giants Existed

Servants's size under the giant people

4. Newspapers Use To Report These Findings All of The Time

"In February and June of 1931, large skeletons were found in the Humboldt lake bed near Lovelock, Nevada. The first of these two skeletons found measured 8 1/2 feet tall and appeared to have been wrapped in a gum-covered fabric similar to the Egyptian manner. The second skeleton was almost 10 feet long." – *Review – Miner*, June 19th, 1931

5. Buffalo Bill Cody Wrote About Giants In His Autobiography

In the autobiography of William "Buffalo Bill" Cody, Cody writes that while camping on the South Platte, a Pawnee Indian came into the camp with what the army surgeon pronounced to be a giant thigh bone of a human being. When Cody asked about where such a bone might have come from, the Indian replied that long ago a race of giants had lived in the area. This race of men had been three times larger than normal men and able to out-run a buffalo and even carry it in one hand.

100 Pics That Prove Nephilim Giants Existed

6. Is The Smithsonian Destroying Important Parts of Our History?

Though the idea of the Smithsonian' covering up a valuable archaeological find is difficult to accept for some, there is, sadly, a great deal of evidence to suggest that the Smithsonian Institution has knowingly covered up and 'lost' important archaeological relics. The STONEWATCH NEWSLETTER of the Gungywamp Society in Connecticut, which researches megalithic sites in New England, had a curious story in their Winter 1992 issue about stone coffins discovered in 1892 in Alabama which were sent to the Smithsonian Institution and then 'lost'.

7. There Are Giant Bones On Display At A Museum In Lima Peru

*Glenn Kimball photographed the mummies of two of these giant men in Lima Peru in 1969. These giants are still in the gold museum in Lima Peru today and can be seen by anyone who visits. They were mummified because their golden robes are prominently on display. Their crowns could fit around Glenn's waist. Their golden gloves have fingers ten inches long. Their mummies can be measured with a tape and they were both around nine and a half feet tall. There were other personal items fit for a giant king, that wouldn't have been useful to a man of normal size. The actual bodies are there e*ncased in glass for all to see. The news media has never photographed anyone nine and a half feet tall.

8. Giants Have Been Found Buried In Kentucky of All Places

"From a mound on the farm of Edin Burrowes, near Franklin, were exhumed, in May, 1841, at a depth of over 12 feet, several human skeletons. One, of extraordinary dimensions, was found between what appeared to have been two logs, covered with a wooden slab.

Many of the bones were entire. The under jaw-bone was large enough to fit over the jaw, flesh and all, of any common man of the present day. The thigh-bones were full six inches longer than those of any man in Simpson County. Teeth, arms, ribs, and all, gave evidence of a giant of a former race". (History of Kentucky, Lewis Collins)

9. Ferdinand of Magallanes and His Crew Encountered Giants

"One day, when no one was expecting it, we saw a giant, completely naked, by the sea. He danced and jumped and, singing, spread sand and dust over his head…He was so tall that the tallest among us reached only to his waist. He was truly well built…The captain named these kind of people Pataghoni. They have no houses but huts, like the Egyptians. They live on raw meat and eat a kind of sweet root which they call capac. The two giants we had on board ship ate their way through a large basket of biscuits, and ate rats without skinning them. They used to drink a half bucket of water at once." – Antonio Pigafetta (1520)

10. Three Giants Were Found Buried In Kentucky

"A few minutes prying served to loosen this and disclose to view the interior of an enclosure in the solid rock of about five by ten feet, which contained the remains of three skeletons, which measure eight feet seven and a half inches, eight feet five inches and eight feet four an three quarter inches in length respectively." – Louisville-Courier-Journal Columbia, Kentucky January 30, 1876

11. Even The Bible Speaks of Giants In Egypt

"And he slew an Egyptian, a man of *great* stature, five cubits high; and in the Egyptian's hand *was* a spear like a weaver's beam; and he went down to him with a staff, and plucked the spear out of the Egyptian's hand, and slew him with his own spear." – 1 Chronicles 11:23

12. Several Giants Were Found In A Mound In Kansas

"It measured sixty-four by thirty-five feet at the summit, gradually sloping in every direction and was eight feet in height. There was found in it a sort of clay coffin including the skeleton of a woman measuring eight feet in length. Within this coffin was found also the skeleton of a child about three and a half feet in length and an image that crumbled when exposed to the atmosphere. In another grave was found the skeleton of a man and a woman, the former measuring nine and the latter eight feet in length. In a third grave occurred two other skeletons, male and female, measuring respectively nine feet four inches and eight feet." – Ancient American Giants, Scientific American, August 14, 1880 Page 106

100 Pics That Prove Nephilim Giants Existed

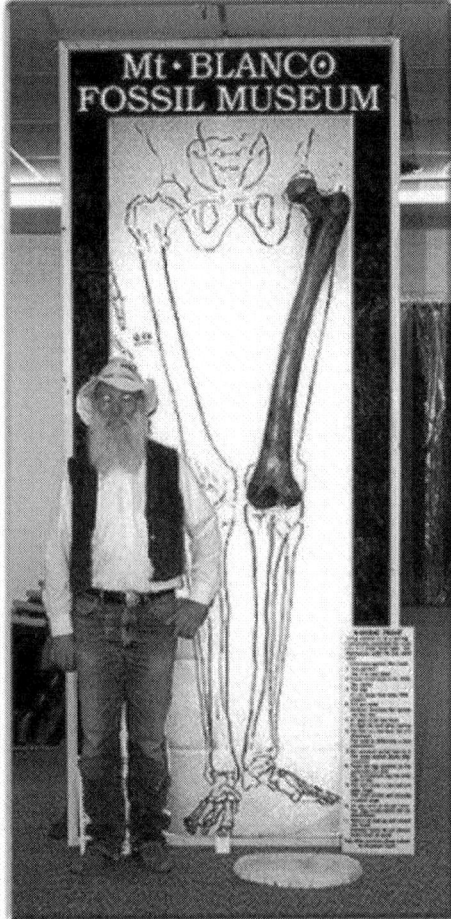

47 inch Human Femur

In the late 1950s, during road construction in south-east Turkey in the Euphrates Valley, many tombs containing the remains of Giants were uncovered. At two sites the leg bones were measured to be about 120 cms "47.24 inches". Joe Taylor, Director of the Mt. BLANCO FOSSIL MUSEUM in Crosbyton, Texas, was commissioned to sculpt this anatomically correct, and to scale, human femur. This "Giant" stood some 14-16 feet tall, and had 20-22 inch long feet. His or Her finger tips, with arms to their sides, would be about 6 feet above the ground. The Biblical record, in Deuteronomy 3:11 states that the Iron Bed of Og, King of Bashan was 9 cubits by 4 cubits or approximately 14 feet long by 6 feet wide!

GENESIS 6:4 —
There were Nephilim (Giants) in the earth in those days; and also after that when the sons of God (Angels?) came in unto the daughters of men, and they bare children to them, the same became mighty men which were of old, men of renown.

More Info & Replicas available at mtblanco1@aol.com or www.mtblanco.com
Mt. Blanco Fossil Museum • P.O. Box 559, Crosbyton, TX 79322 • 1-800-367-7454

13. Legends of Giant Cannibals Are Found All Over The World

"The giant's name was Oo-el-en. They were vicious giants for they liked to eat the meat of the Indians. Oo-el-en would catch the adults and carry them away to a hiding place near the foot of Cascade Falls. Oo-el-en would then cut the people into small pieces, hanging their meat in the sun to dry into jerky. The legend says that the Ahwahneechees finally killed the giants and burned their bodies." – Ahwahneechees Legend

14. Amerigo Vespucci Claimed He Encountered Giants

"They were such large women that we were about determining to carry off two of the younger ones as a present to our king; but while we were debating this subject, thirty-six men entered the hut where we were drinking. They were of such great stature that each one was taller when upon his knees than I when standing erect. In fact, they were giants; each of the women appeared a Penthesilia, and the men Antei. When they came in, some of our number were so frightened that they did not consider themselves safe, for they were armed with very large bows and arrows, besides immense clubs made in the form of swords."

34. A group of natives in the central highlands of Mexico, capturing and putting to death a giant. From the Codex Vaticano A, 8v

15. Charles Debrosses Encountered Brazilian Giants

"The coast of Port Desire is inhabited by giants fifteen to sixteen palms high. I have myself measured the footprint of one of them on the riverbank, which was four times longer than one of ours. I have also measured the corpses of two men recently buried by the river, which were fourteen spans long. Three of our men, who were later taken by the Spanish on the coast of Brazil, assured me that one day on the other side of the coast they had to sail out to sea because the giants started throwing great blocks of stone of astonishing size from the beach right at their boat. In Brazil I saw one of these giants which Alonso Diaz had captured at Port Saint Julien: he was just a boy but was already thirteen spans tall."

16. Captain John Byron Encountered Giants

"In 1767 Captain John Byron and the H.M.S. Dolphin returned to port and published "Voyage Round the World in His Majesty's Ship the Dolphin" in his book he hailed the voyage as "…putting an end to the dispute, which for two centuries and a half has subsisted between geographers, in relation to the reality of there being a nation of people of such an amazing stature, of which the concurrent testimony of all on board the Dolphin and Tamer can now leave no room for doubt. "

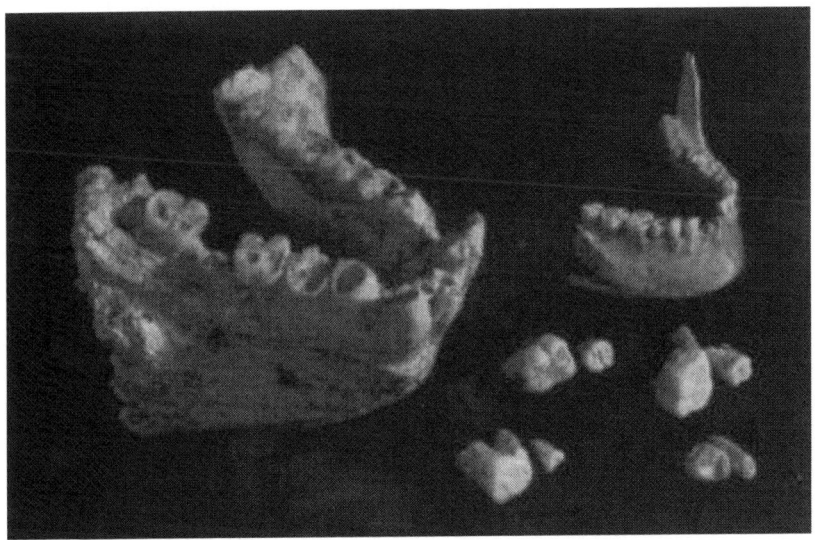

17. New York Tribune Reports Giant Find In 1909

"A peon while excavating for the foundation of a house on the estate of Augustin Juarez found the skeleton of a human being that is estimated to have been about 15 feet high, and who must have lived ages ago, judging from the ossified state of the bones... The discovery of the skeleton has revived the old Aztec legend that in a prehistoric age a race of giants lived valley of Anahuac, a name given by the aboriginal Mexicans to that part of the Mexican plateau nearly corresponding to the modern valley of Mexico City. These giants, known as Quinatzins, the story goes, were afterwards destroyed by the Ulmecas, also of great stature, who in turn, perished by earthquake, interpreted as an expression of the wrath of God."

100 Pics That Prove Nephilim Giants Existed

18. The Israelites Were Scared of Giants

"Whither shall we go up? our brethren have discouraged our heart, saying, the people are greater and taller than we; the cities are great and walled up to heaven; and moreover we have seen the sons of the Anakims there" – Deuteronomy 1:28

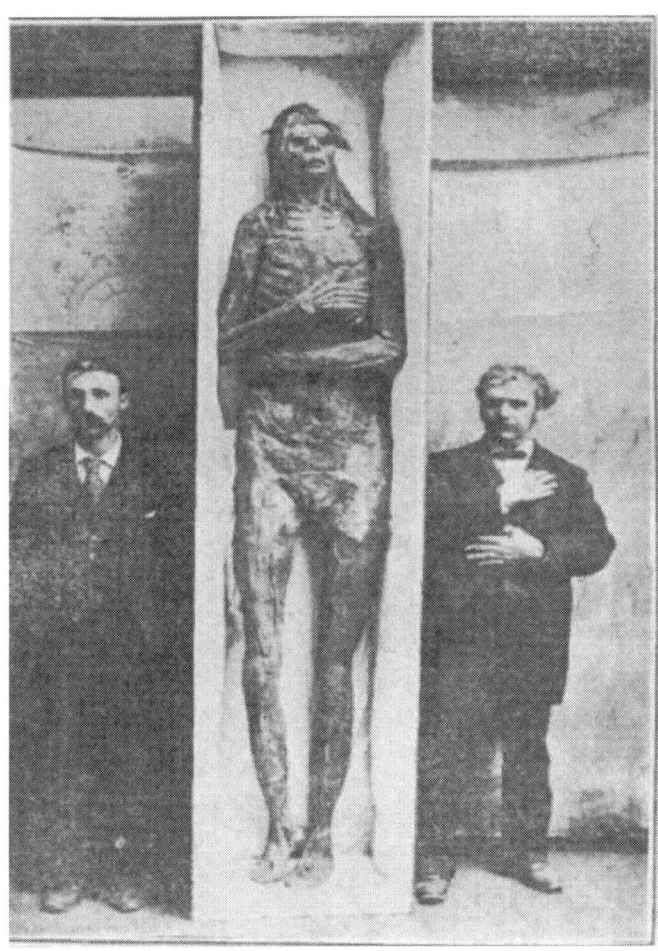

19. King Og's Bed Was Over 14 Feet Long and 6 Feet Wide

"For only Og king of Bashan remained of the remnant of giants; behold his bedstead was a bedstead of iron; is it not in Rabbath of the children of Ammon? nine cubits was the length thereof, and four cubits the breadth of it, after the cubit of a man." – Deuteronomy 3:11

20. The Sumerians Believed In Giants As Well

"Gilgamesh and Enkidu go together to fight the evil Humbaba at the cedar mountains. The evil giants face was like a lion, a roar like a flood, a mouth of flames, breath that burns trees, and teeth like a dragons. In the end they cut off his head." – Epic of Gilgamesh (summary)

100 Pics That Prove Nephilim Giants Existed

21. The Spartans Believed In Giants

"The Spartans uncovered in Tegea the body of Orestes which was seven cubits long — around 10 feet. In his book, 'The Comparison of Romulus with Theseus' Plutarch describes how the Athenians uncovered the body of Theseus, which was of more than ordinary size. The kneecaps of Ajax were exactly the size of a discus for the boy's pentathlon, wrote Pausanias. A boy's discus was about twelve centimetres in diameter, while a normal adult patella is around five centimetres, suggesting Ajax may have been around 14 feet tall." – Herodotus in Book 1, Chapter 68

22. Pliny Makes A Reference To Giants

"The Arabian giant Gabara was 9 feet 9 inches. This Arabian giant was the tallest man seen in the days of Claudius." – Pliny

23. 90 Foot Tall Giant Believed To Have Existed

"Antæos is 60 cubits in height. The grave of the giant was opened by Serbon." – Plutarch

24. Giants Once Roamed Australia

"Throughout the length and breadth of central and far western New South wales, Aboriginal traditions speak of the Bulloo, or 'giant men and women', who they claim were 3m tall beings who wandered the land eating giant marsupials and other Australian ice-age 'megafauna' which they killed with large stone clubs and other giant-size implements. Further to the east, there dwelt the 'Jogungs' and 'Goolagahs', or 'giant hairy ones', tool making giant hominids sometimes confused with the Yowies, and who may, or may not have been related to the Bulloo." – Australia Legend

25. The Norse Had A Heave Belief In Giants

"In the Norse world, a giant was called Jotun or Iotun. There are several different types of giants. The frost-giants were the most common giants; they lived in Jotunheim, one of the nine worlds. The capital of Jotunheim was Utgard, the citadel of the frost-giants and home of Utgard-Loki or Utgardaloki. Often writers just simply called the home of the giants as Giantland." – Norse Legend

26. The Hindu Religion Believes In Giants

"In Hinduism, the giants are called Daityas. They were a race who fought against the gods because they were jealous of their Deva half-brothers. Some Daityas from Hindu mythology include Kumbhakarna and Hiranyaksha." – Hindu Legend

100 Pics That Prove Nephilim Giants Existed

27. Little John Is Often Depicted As A Giant

"There is some debate regarding the existence of Robin Hood and his band of merry men, the most massive of whom was the legendary Little John. Most stories indicate he was at least seven feet tall, which would have been more massive by far than any of his 13th century countrymen."

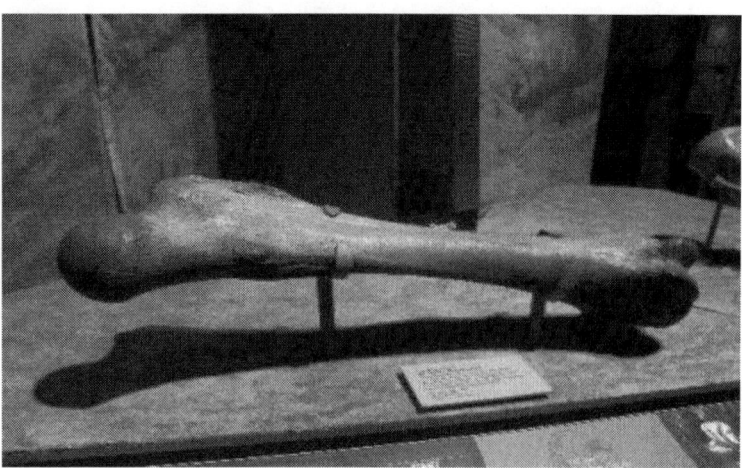

28. Legends of Giants Live On In The Modern Day

"Yeti, the Abominable Snowman of Tibet, Yerin, the Wildman of China, and Sasquatch, the Big Foot of America, are all mysterious giants who live in the mountains. There are many stories of sightings or attacks by these mysterious creatures."

WISCONSIN MOUND OPENED.

Skeleton Found of a Man Over Nine Feet High with an Enormous Skull.

MAPLE CREEK, Wis., Dec. 19.—One of the three recently discovered mounds in this town has been opened. In it was found the skeleton of a man of gigantic size. The bones measured from head to foot over nine feet and were in a fair state of preservation. The skull was as large as a half bushel measure. Some finely tempered rods of copper and other relics were lying near the bones.

The mound from which these relics were taken is ten feet high and thirty feet long, and varies from six to eight feet in width.

The two mounds of lesser size will be excavated soon.

The New York Times
Published: December 20, 1897
Copyright © The New York Times

29. The Cyclopes Were Giant Shepherds In Sicily

"The Cyclopes were a tribe of one-eyed cannibalistic giants who shepherded flocks of sheep on the island of Sicily. One of them was Polyphemus who captured Odysseus and his men, but was later blinded and tricked by the hero."

30. Chenoos Were Man Eating Giants of Wabanaki Indian Legend

"Chenoos are the evil man-eating ice giants of northern Wabanaki legends. A Chenoo was once a human being who either became possessed by an evil spirit or committed a terrible crime (especially cannibalism or withholding food from a starving person), causing his heart to turn to ice. In a few legends a human has been successfully rescued from the frozen heart of a Chenoo, but usually once a person has been transformed into a Chenoo, their only escape is death."

31. Lofa: The Man Eating Chickasaw Giant

"The Lofa is a malevolent, ogre-like monster of Chickasaw folklore. His name literally means "flayer" or "skinner," a reference to his gruesome habit of flaying the skin from his victims. In some legends he attempts to abduct Chickasaw women. He is sometimes described as a giant and other times as a large, hairy, smelly man, leading some people to associate him with the Bigfoot legend."

> **FIND GIANT INDIANS' BONES.**
>
> **Workmen on Harlem Road Unearth Relics of Teekus Tribe.**
>
> *Special to The New York Times.*
>
> KATONAH, N. Y., Sept. 6.—While a gang of men in the employ of the New York and Harlem Railroad were taking sand from an immense mound near Purdy's Station today to fill in an excavation, they unearthed several skeletons of unusual size.
>
> The bones are believed to be those of Indians who once lived in this vicinity and belonged to a tribe that was led by the great Chief Teekus, from whom the Titicus Valley, now a part of the New York watershed, takes its name. Besides finding the bones, the workmen also exhumed a score or more of arrowheads, hatchets, and copper implements. It is believed that the large mound in which the relics were found was once the burying ground of the Teekus Indians. The last Indians were seen in the valley a short time after the Revolutionary War.
>
> The bones found to-day were brought to Katonah and will be reinterred in the local cemetery.
>
> *The New York Times*
> Published: September 7, 1904
> Copyright © The New York Times

32. Stone Coat Is A Man Eating Giant of Iroquois Indian Legend

"Stone Coat is the name of a mythological rock giant of the Iroquois-speaking tribes. In some tribal traditions there is only one Stone Coat, while in others, there is a whole race of them. Stone Coats are described as being about twice as tall as humans, with their bodies covered in rock-hard scales that repel all normal weapons. They are associated with winter and ice, and they hunt and eat humans."

100 Pics That Prove Nephilim Giants Existed

33. Kuku Was A Man Eating Female Giant of Mi'kmaq Legend

"The Kuku or Gougou is a kind of man-eating giant, usually (but not always) described as female. Gougou is so huge that she carries the people she catches in a bag over her shoulder the way human hunters carry rabbits. The Mi'kmaq name Kuku may derive from their word for "earthquake," *kiwkw*, since she is so large her footsteps shake the earth."

34. The Daituas Were Giants of Hindu Mythology

"They were a race of giants who fought against the Devas because they were jealous of their Deva half-brothers. The female Daityas are described as wearing jewelry the size of boulders"

GIANT SKELETONS FOUND.

Archaeologists to Send Expedition to Explore Graveyards in New Mexico Where Bodies Were Unearthed.

Special to The New York Times.

LOS ANGELES, Cal., Feb. 10.—Owing to the discovery of the remains of a race of giants in Guadalupe, N. M., antiquarians and archaeologists are preparing an expedition further to explore that region. This determination is based on the excitement that exists among the people of a scope of country near Mesa Rico, about 200 miles southeast of Las Vegas, where an old burial ground has been discovered that has yielded skeletons of enormous size.

Luiciana Quintana, on whose ranch the ancient burial plot is located, discovered two stones that bore curious inscriptions, and beneath these were found in shallow excavations the bones of a frame that could not have been less than 12 feet in length. The men who opened the grave say the forearm was 4 feet long and that in a well-preserved jaw the lower teeth ranged from the size of a hickory nut to that of the largest walnut in size.

The chest of the being is reported as having a circumference of seven feet.

Quintana, who has uncovered many other burial places, expresses the opinion that perhaps thousands of skeletons of a race of giants long extinct will be found. This supposition is based on the traditions handed down from the early Spanish invasion that have detailed knowledge of the existence of a race of giants that inhabited the plains of what now is Eastern New Mexico. Indian legends and carvings also in the same section indicate the existence of such a race.

The New York Times
Published: February 11, 1902
Copyright © The New York Times

35. The Jentil Were Stone Throwing Giants of Basque Mythology

"The Jentil, were a race of giants in the Basque mythology. This word meaning *gentile*, from Latin *gentilis*, was used to refer to prechristian civilizations and in particular to the builders of megalithic monuments"

More Big Indians Found in Virginia.

Not to be behind Canada, Virginia puts in a claim of the possession of a cave full of dead Indians, the Petersburg *Index* giving the tale as quoted below, on the authority of gentlemen whom it asserts to be of the highest character and credit, who have seen with their own eyes, and touched and tested with their own hands, the wonderful objects of which they make report as follows:

"The workmen engaged in opening a way for the projected railroad between Weldon and Garysburg struck Monday, about one mile from the former place, in a bank beside the river, a catacomb of skeletons, supposed to be those of Indians, of a remote age and a lost and forgotten race. The bodies exhumed were of strange and remarkable formation. The skulls were nearly an inch in thickness; the teeth were filed sharp, as are those of cannibals, the enamel perfectly preserved; the bones were of wonderful length and strength—the *femur* being as long as the leg of an ordinary man, the stature of the body being, probably, as great as eight or nine feet. Near their heads were sharp stone arrows, stone mortars, in which their corn was brayed, and the bowls of pipes, apparently of soft friable soap-stone. The teeth of the skeletons are said to be as large as those of horses. One of them has been brought to the city, and presented to an officer of the Petersburg Railroad. The bodies were found closely packed together, laid tier on tier as it seemed. There was no discernable ingress into or egress out of the mound."

The New York Times
Published: September 8, 1871

36. The Bible Is Full of Tribes of Giants Inhabiting Canaan

"The Emims dwelt therein in times past, a people great, and many, and tall, as the Anakims; Which also were accounted giants, as the Anakims; but the Moabites call them Emims." – Deuteronomy 2:10-11

MAY BE RELATED TO CARDIFF GIANT

Bones of a Human Skeleton Eleven Feet High Are Dug Up in Nevada.

WINNEMUCCA, Nev., Jan. 23.— Workmen engaged in digging gravel here today uncovered at a depth of about twelve feet a lot of bones, part of the skeleton of a gigantic human being.

Dr. Samuels examined them and pronounced them to be the bones of a man who must have been nearly eleven feet in height.

The metacarpal bones measure four and a half inches in length and are large in proportion. A part of the ulna was found and in its complete form would have been between seventeen and eighteen inches in length.

The remainder of the skeleton is being searched for.

The Saint Paul globe., January 24, 1904

37. Were The Man Eating Giants of Paiute Legend s True?

"The Paiutes named the giants Si-Te-Cah that literally means "tule-eaters." The tule is a fibrous water plant the giants wove into rafts to escape the Paiutes continuous attacks. They used the rafts to navigate across what remained of Lake Lahontan. The Paiutes named the giants Si-Te-Cah that literally means "tule-eaters." The tule is a fibrous water plant the giants wove into rafts to escape the Paiutes continuous attacks. They used the rafts to navigate across what remained of Lake Lahontan."

SKULLS OF GIANT CAVEMEN

many of these caves. At a depth of more than three feet he found the remains of several giant human skeletons, including an almost perfect skull which differed in many particulars from a modern specimen. When partly joined the largest skeleton was almost ten feet tall.

The New age magazine: Volume 18 Page 207 - 1913

38. Homer Said The Following About Giants

"On the earth there once were giants." – Greek poet Homer, 400 B.C.E.

GIANTS' SKELETONS FOUND.

Cave in Mexico Gives Up the Bones of an Ancient Race.

Special to The New York Times.

BOSTON, May 3.—Charles C. Clapp, who has recently returned from Mexico, where he has been in charge of Thomas W. Lawson's mining interests, has called the attention of Prof. Agassiz to a remarkable discovery made by him.

He found in Mexico a cave containing some 200 skeletons of men each above eight feet in height. The cave was evidently the burial place of a race of giants who antedated the Aztecs. Mr. Clapp arranged the bones of one of these skeletons and found the total length to be 8 feet 11 inches. The femur reached up to his thigh, and the molars were big enough to crack a cocoanut. The head measured eighteen inches from front to back.

The New York Times
Published: May 4, 1908
Copyright © The New York Times

39. The Word "Giant" Originates From Greek Mythology

"In Greek mythology the gigantes were (according to the poet Hesiod) the children of Uranos and Gaea (The Heaven and the Earth). They were involved in a conflict with the Olympian gods called the Gigantomachy, which was eventually settled when the hero Heracles decided to help the Olympians."

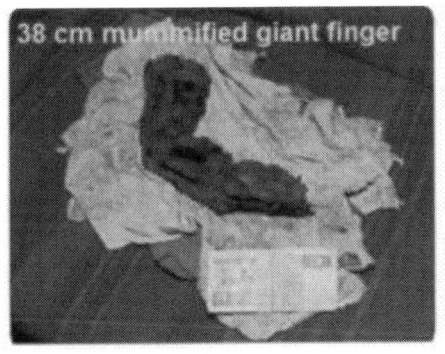

40. The Israelites Fought Giants In The Promised Land

"That also was accounted a land of giants: giants dwelt therein in old time; and the Ammonites call them Zamzummims;" – Deuteronomy 2:20

A Race of Giants in Old Gaul.

From the London Globe.

In the year 1890 some human bones of enormous size, double the ordinary in fact, were found in the tumulus of Castelnau, (Hérault,) and have since been carefully examined by Prof. Kiener, who, while admitting that the bones are those of a very tall race, nevertheless finds them abnormal in dimensions and apparently of morbid growth. They undoubtedly reopen the question of the "giants" of antiquity, but do not furnish sufficient evidence to decide it.

The New York Times
Published: October 3, 1892
Copyright © The New York Times

41. Sumerian Giants Are Described The Same As Biblical Giants

"The earliest known organized culture is thought to be the **Sumerians** in the Mesopotamia Valley. They have left behind stone tablets depicting life at the time. Many of those carved images depict the *"Giant Kings,"* men with six fingers, perhaps 12 to 18 feet tall, that the citizens are bowing down to and worshiping."

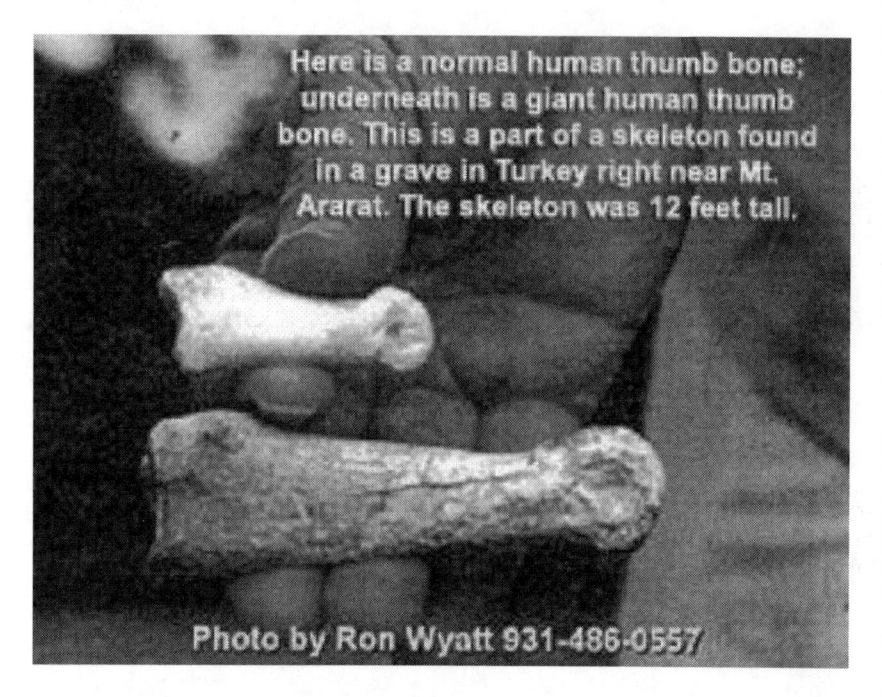

Here is a normal human thumb bone; underneath is a giant human thumb bone. This is a part of a skeleton found in a grave in Turkey right near Mt. Ararat. The skeleton was 12 feet tall.

Photo by Ron Wyatt 931-486-0557

42. Jack The Giant Killer Was Believed To Be A Real Person

"Welsh folklore and legend produced *Ye Olde' English Tales* of Jack the Giant Killer. There were several tales besides the *"beanstalk"* tale most are familiar with. Jack had battles and skirmishes with giants, *Cormoran* and *Blunderbore"*

43. A Giant Skeleton Was Discovered In Virginia

"A decayed human skeleton claimed by eyewitnesses to measure around 3.28 metres (10 feet 9 inches tall), was unearthed by laborers while plowing a vineyard in November 1856 in East Wheeling, now in West Virginia."

THREE SKELETONS OF OLDEN GIANTS ARE DISCOVERED

Road-workers at Waimea, Hawaii, Dig Up Bones of Men Over Seven Feet Tall

LEGEND OF GREAT BATTLE BELIEVED NOW CONFIRMED

Story of Maui King Whose Bodyguard Fell on Invasion, Brought Back to Mind

AND SO THEY WERE PROBABLY INDEED "SECURED" AND NEVER SEEN AGAIN, LET ALONE DISPLAYED IN ANY BISHOP MUSEUM!

3 Giant Skeletons over 7 Feet Tall Waimea 1912 Newspaper.

44. A Giant Skeleton Was Discovered In California

"A human skeleton measuring 3.6 metres (12 foot) tall was unearthed at Lompock Rancho, California, in 1833 by soldiers digging in a pit for a powder magazine. The specimen had a double row of teeth and was surrounded by numerous stone axes, carved shells and porphyry blocks with abstruse symbols associated with it."

45. The Bible Speaks of The Land of The Giants

"And the rest of Gilead, and all Bashan, *being* the kingdom of Og, gave I unto the half tribe of Manasseh; all the region of Argob, with all Bashan, which was called the land of giants." – Deuteronomy 3:13

46. A Giant Skeleton Has Been Found In Louisiana

"A 9' 11" skeleton was unearthed in 1928 by a farmer digging a pit to bury trash in Tensas Parish, Louisiana near Waterproof. In 1931 a 10' 2" skeleton was unearthed by a boy burying his dog in 1933 in Nearby Madison Parish."

47. A Giant Skeleton Was Discovered In Indiana

"9' 8" skeleton was excavated from a mound near Brewersville, Indiana (Indianapolis News, Nov 10, 1975)."

100 Pics That Prove Nephilim Giants Existed

48. A Giant Human Skeleton Was Discovered In Minnesota

"In Clearwater Minnesota, the skeletons of seven giants were found in mounds. These had receding foreheads and complete double dentition (Childress 1992, p. 468)."

Giants of Egypt

49. Moses and Joshua Killed Giants In The Promised Land

"All the kingdom of Og in Bashan, which reigned in Ashtaroth and in Edrei, who remained of the remnant of the giants: for these did Moses smite, and cast them out." – Joshua 13:12

100 Pics That Prove Nephilim Giants Existed

50. Multiple Giant Skeletons Were Discovered In Ohio

"A mound near Toledo, Ohio, held 20 skeletons, seated and facing east with jaws and teeth "twice as large as those of present day people," and besides each was a large bowl with "curiously wrought hieroglyphic figures." (Chicago Record, Oct. 24, 1895; cited by Ron G. Dobbins, NEARA Journal, v13, fall 1978)."

51. Giants Were Believed To Have Been The First Masons

"In all the existing remains of Cyclopean architecture…there is a singular resemblance for which it is difficult to account. It has been suggested that the Cyclopeans were a kind of Freemasons employed to construct lighthouses, citadels, &c., who handed down their mysterious art from generation to generation; and that the stupendous nature of their edifices led to the fables with which the name is associated." —Charles Boileau Elliott, Travels in the three great empires of Austria, Russia, and Turkey, Volume 2 (1838)

52. A 12 Foot Tall Giant Was Discovered In 1833

"In 1833, soldiers digging at Lompock Rancho, California, discovered a male skeleton 12 feet tall. The skeleton was surrounded by caved shells, stone axes, other artifacts. The skeleton had double rows of upper and lower teeth. Unfortunately, this body was secretly buried because the local Indians became upset about the remains."

Giant guy puts his hands on the boat

53. Giant Footprints Were Found In New Mexico In 1932

"In 1932, Ellis Wright found human tracks in the gypsum rock at White Sands, New Mexico. His discovery was later backed up by Fred Arthur, Supervisor of the Lincoln National Park and others who reported that each footprint was 22 inches long and from 8 to 10 inches wide. They were certain the prints were human in origin due to the outline of the perfect prints coupled with a readily apparent instep."

54. A Giant Attempted To Assassinate King David

"And Ishbibenob, which *was* of the sons of the giant, the weight of whose spear *weighed* three hundred *shekels* of brass in weight, he being girded with a new *sword*, thought to have slain David." – 2 Samuel 21:16

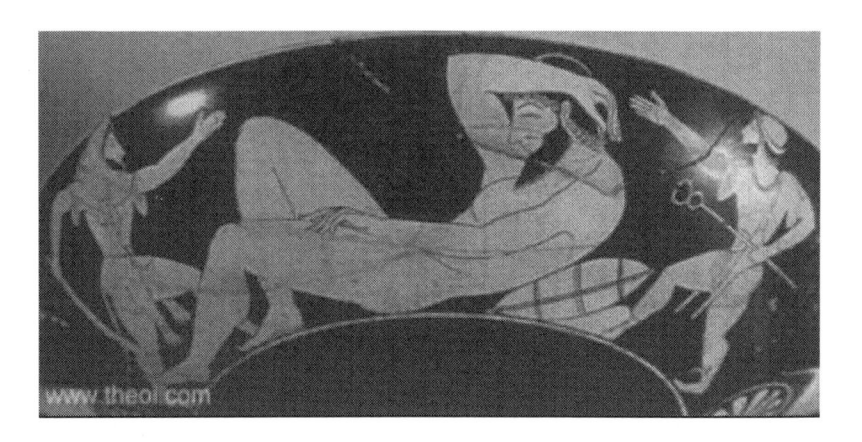

55. Giant Remains Discovered During WWII

"During World War II, author Ivan T. Sanderson tells of how his crew was bulldozing through sedimentary rock when it stumbled upon what appeared to be a graveyard. In it were crania that measured from 22 to 24 inches from base to crown nearly three times as large as an adult human skull. Had the creatures to whom these skulls belonged been properly proportioned, they undoubtedly would have been at least 12 feet tall or taller."

56. Was St. Christopher A Cannibalistic Giant?

"One of the latest accounts of a race of giants that occupied Europe comes from the middle ages and involves a surprising figure: Saint Christopher. While modern stories of St. Christopher simply make him out as an ordinary man, or perhaps a somewhat homely man, those who actually saw him had a different story. According to his peers, he was a giant, belonging to a tribe of dog-headed, cannibalistic giants. Jacques de Voragine in The Golden Legend wrote of St. Christopher:"He was of gigantic stature, had a terrifying mien, was twelve coudees tall."

57. David Wasn't The Only Man To Kill A Giant In The Bible

"And it came to pass after this, that there was again a battle with the Philistines at Gob: then Sibbechai the Hushathite slew Saph, which *was* of the sons of the giant." – 2 Samuel 21:18

58. Celtic Giants Have a Legendary History

"Not a lot is known about the people who would become known as the Celts. It is known that they migrated across Asia Minor, through northern Europe and into what have become the Celtic countries of Wales, Scotland and Ireland. Most accounts of them include references to the giants that were often found among them. The ancient Greek historian Pausanias called them "the world's tallest people."

59. Was The Nazi Idea of A Super Race Inspired By Giants?

"The travels of the giants through the German region also most likely inspired the Teutonic legends of the Aryan race of superhumans (with the early name of "Cimmerian" having an obvious resemblance that is probably more than happenstance to Aryan). The Nazi ideal "superman" was a blue-eyed, blond giant; this is the exact historic description of the Celtae. DeLoach has also made a good argument that the giants ruling the Celtae may very well have been descendants of the Anakim, the giants the Israelites found in the Promised Land."

60. Legends of Six Digit Giants Exist All Over The World

"And there was yet a battle in Gath, where was a man of *great* stature, that had on every hand six fingers, and on every foot six toes, four and twenty in number; and he also was born to the giant." – 2 Samuel 21:20

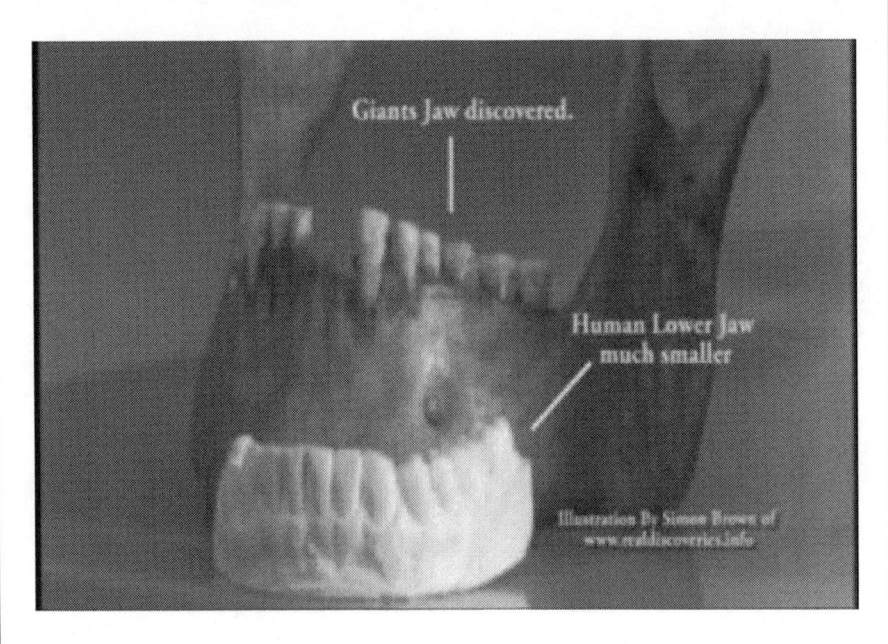

61. Sources Claim Homosexuality Was Normal Among Giants

"Although their wives are comely, they have very little to do with them, but rage with lust in outlandish fashion for the embraces of males. And the most astonishing thing of all is that they feel no concern for their proper dignity but prostitute to others without a qualm the flower of their bodies; nor do they consider this a disgraceful thing to do, but rather when anyone of them is thus approached and refuses the favor offered him, this they consider an act of dishonor."

62. The Book of Enoch Speaks of The Origin of Giants

"Then they (the angels) took wives, each choosing for himself, whom they began to approach, and with whom they cohabited;

teaching them sorcery, incantations, and the divining of roots and trees. And the women conceiving brought forth giants…"

63. The Book of Jubilees Also Tells The Origin of Giants

"…that the angels of God saw them (earthly women) on a certain year of this jubilee, that they were beautiful to look upon; and they took themselves wives of all whom they chose, and they bare to them sons and they were giants. …"

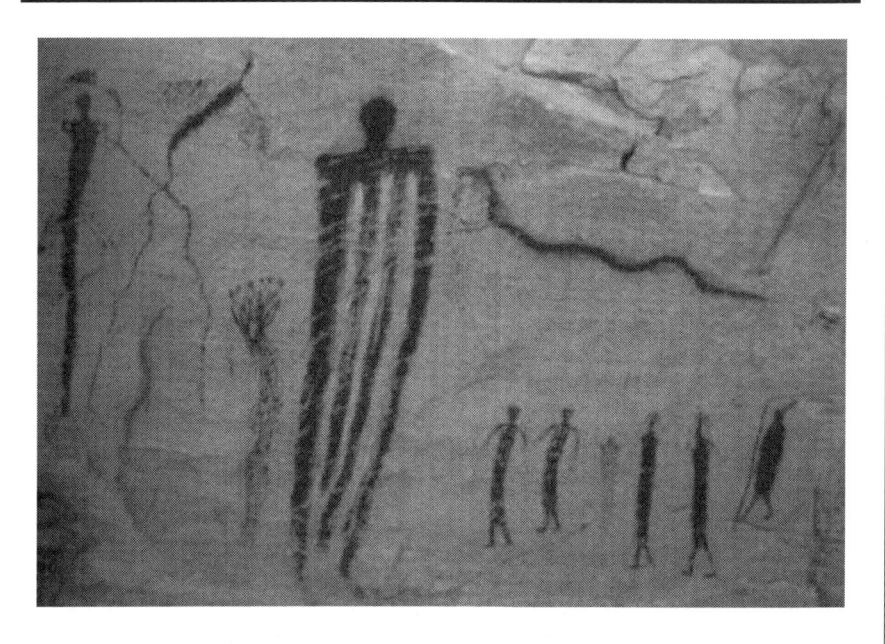

64. Were Giants The First To Dabble In Genetic Manipulation?

"And their judges and rulers (which were the giants at this time) went to the daughters of men and took their wives by force from their husbands according to their choice, and son of men of those days took from the cattle of the earth, the beasts of field, and fowls of the air, and taught the mixture of animals of one species with the other, in order therewith to provoke the Lord; and God saw that the whole earth and it was corrupt, for all flesh had corrupted its ways upon earth, all men and all animals." – The Book of Jasher

65. There Were At Least Five Giants In Gath During David's Reign

"These four were born to the giant in Gath, and fell by the hand of David, and by the hand of his servants." – 2 Samuel 21:20

66. Did Giants Travel To Peru By Boat?

I have stated above that the Peruvians preserved no record of having come originally from China. They had a tradition, however, concerning certain foreigners who came by sea to their country, which may be worth repeating; Garcilasso de la Vega gives this tradition as he himself heard it in Peru. They affirm, he says, in all Peru, that certain giants came by sea to the cape now called St Helens, in large barks made of rushes. These giants were so enor-

mously tall that ordinary men reached no higher than their knees."
– The Works of Huburt Howe Bancroft, Vol., 5 Native Races 1882

67. The Roman Emperor Maximinus Thrax Was A Giant

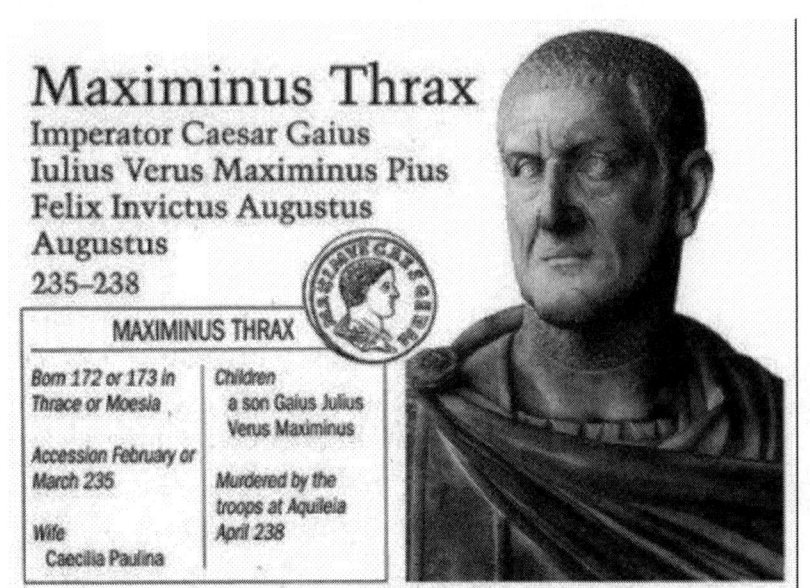

Maximinus Thrax
Imperator Caesar Gaius
Iulius Verus Maximinus Pius
Felix Invictus Augustus
Augustus
235–238

MAXIMINUS THRAX	
Born 172 or 173 in Thrace or Moesia	Children a son Gaius Julius Verus Maximinus
Accession February or March 235	Murdered by the troops at Aquileia April 238
Wife Caecilia Paulina	

Maximinus was probably the biggest man ever to hold the office of Roman emperor. The Historia Augusta has it that he was <u>8 ft 6 in</u> (2.6 m) tall, and so strong that he could pull laden carts unaided! The size of his footwear was also legendary, and the expression 'Maximinus's boot' came to be used in popular parlance for any tall or lanky individual. Surviving portrait busts, such as this one from the Louvre, show Maximinus as a heavily-muscled man with powerful jaw and close-cropped hair, the image of a seasoned soldier. Not for him the meditative, spiritual pose favoured by Alexander Severus.

Rumored To Have Been Built By Giants

The following well known and lesser known megalithic structures are rumored to have been built by giants. Even with all over our modern knowledge, science still has not offered any reasonable explanation as to how these were constructed.

68. The Great Pyramid – Egypt

69. Baalbek – Lebanon

"The Romans have left us many writings, but none of them describe how they built the site. However, the local population of the Beqa'a Valley still has some knowledge of its origins. They say that Cain, the son of Adam, built a city there before the Great Flood. This place was destroyed during the deluge, but later a race of giants built it up again. Heading this project was Nimrod, the king of Shinar mentioned in the Book of Genesis." – Baalbek local legend

70. Giant's Causeway – Ireland

"Legend says that rivals Finn McCool of County Antrim in Ireland, and the Giant Bennandoner of Scotland were constantly bickering from afar. One day Finn McCool decided to build a bridge to cross the sea and challenge Bennandoner to a fight. He ran across the causeway from Ireland to Scotland to sneak up on Bennadoner, but when he got a closer look at the giant, he discovered that he was larger than he imagined. McCool quickly turned around and ran back to Antrim."

71. Gilgal Refaim – Golan Heights

"In Hebrew the site is called "Wheel of Refaim" because, according to the Tanakh, the ancient people who lived in what is now Golan were actually giants that were called "Rephaites". The term "Galgal" means wheel, and was given due to the site's circular shape. The structure is supposed to be the grave of the last king of the giants."

100 Pics That Prove Nephilim Giants Existed

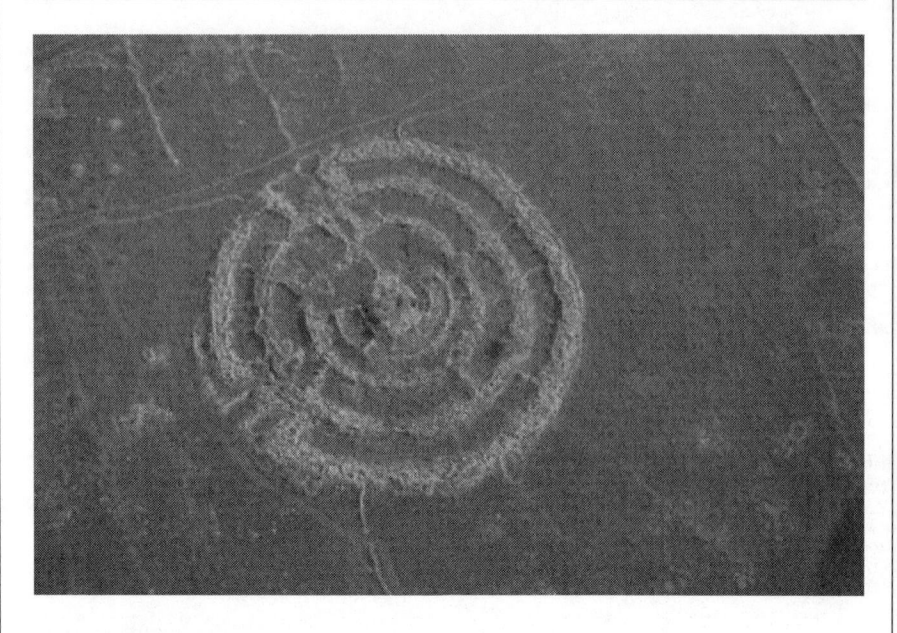

72. Teotihuacan Citadel

73. Sachsayhuaman – Peru

74. Dolmens – Caucuses

75. Orcadian Stones

76. Stonehenge – Great Britain

According to legend, a giant helped Merlin build Stonehenge. "A giant helps Merlin build Stonehenge. From a manuscript of the Roman de Brut [1100s] by Wace in the British Library (Egerton 3028). This is the oldest known depiction of Stonehenge."

100 Pics That Prove Nephilim Giants Existed

77. Petra – Jordan

78. Giant Pharaohs – Nubia

79. Megalithic Stone Monument – Europe

80. The Colossus – Egypt

Might Be Real But Could Be Fake

There were a few pics that looked like the real thing, but I'm a bit skeptical about them, so I figured I'd give them their own special section just to be on the safe side. Let me also be clear that I'm skeptical about the potential for Photoshop and if they really exist, are they actual bones and not plaster or something else?

81. The Swedish Had Their Own Legends of Giants

"The Stallo were portrayed as big stupid giants who caused trouble, ate the people and tormented them, but through good behavior, bravery, and intelligence, the Saami could survive." – University of Texas

100 Pics That Prove Nephilim Giants Existed

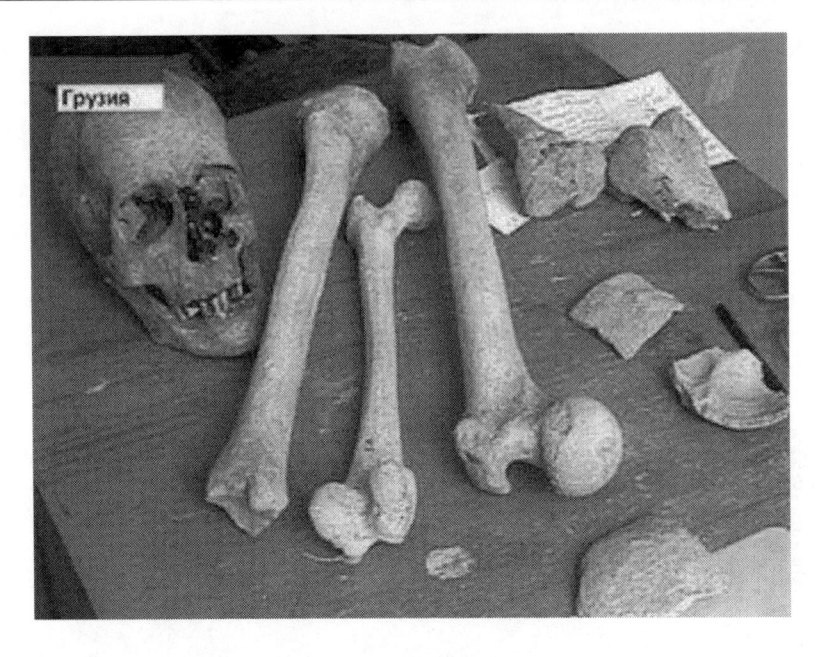

82. These Skulls Look Like The Real Deal

"For many angels of God accompanied with women, and begat sons that proved unjust, and despisers of all that was good, on account of the confidence they had in their own strength; for the tradition is, that these men did what resembled the acts of those whom the Grecians call giants." – Josephus

83. This South African Footprint Is Believed To Be Genuine

"For which reason they removed their camp to Hebron; and when they had taken it, they slew all the inhabitants. There were till then left the race of giants, who had bodies so large, and countenances so entirely different from other men, that they were surprising to the sight, and terrible to the hearing. The bones of these men are still shown to this very day, unlike to any credible relations of other men. Now they gave this city to the Levites as an extraordinary reward..." – Josephus

84. This Looks Similar To The Thigh Bone In The Museum Photo

"The Kai of New Guinea recalled a race of demigods, or giants called the Ne-Mu. They were said to be taller and stronger than the mortal race of today, but they were lords of the earth before the Great Flood. They taught the Kai ancestors the fundamentals of agriculture and house-construction. The Ne-Mu was wiped out during the Deluge, but their bodies transformed into blocks of stone."

85. The Top Center Skull Seems To Stand Out More

"Arabic myth describes a race of giants known as the Adites. These beings are the equivalent of the Atlantean Titans of Greek mythology, and are described as superior architects and builders. Since their earliest recorded history, Arabs in the Middle East have associated all immense structures with these great giants of antiquity."

86. Definitely Real But May Not Be From Giants

87. The Print Looks Too Perfect But May Be Real

100 Pics That Prove Nephilim Giants Existed

88. This Fossilized Finger Could Be From A Normal Human

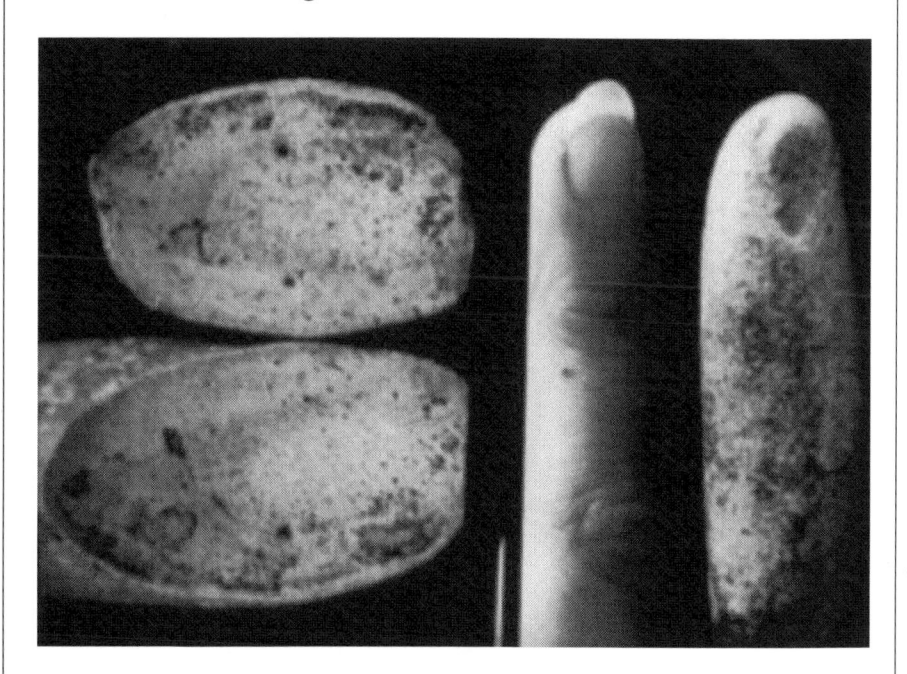

89. This Footprint Seems Oddly Shaped and Possibly Fake

Don't Be Fooled By These Fakes

Wherever there are money and fame to be had, there will always be people that want to pull the wool over our eyes in order to achieve it. The following pics are fakes that have fooled many people over the years.

90. Skeptics Want To Discredit The Real Findings

91. Skeptics Like To Address The Fakes But Avoid The Real Pics

100 Pics That Prove Nephilim Giants Existed

92. This Fake Fooled A Lot of People But Its Exposed Now

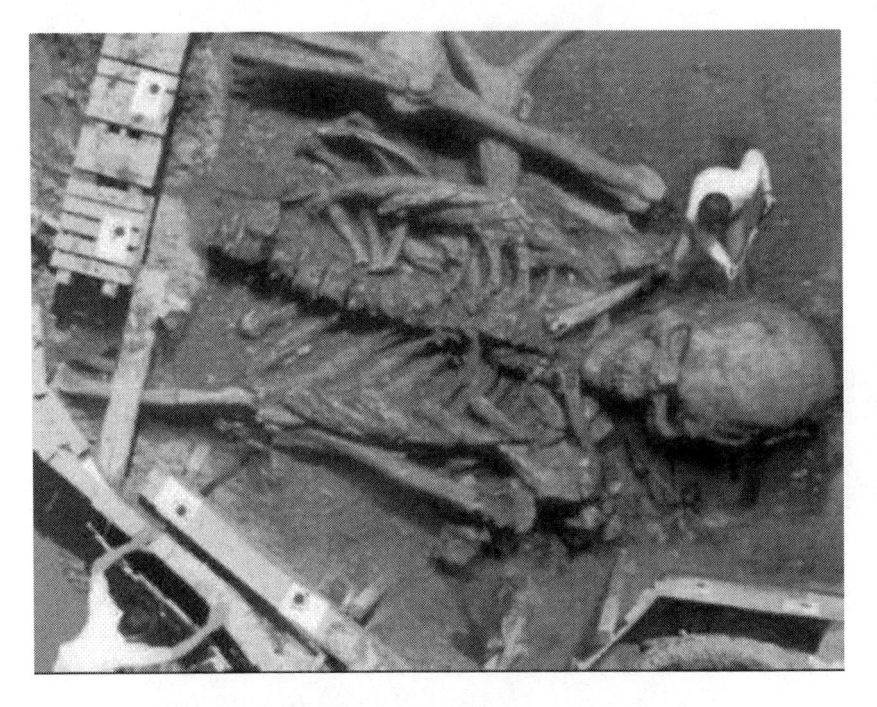

93. A Convincing Pic But Definitely A Fake

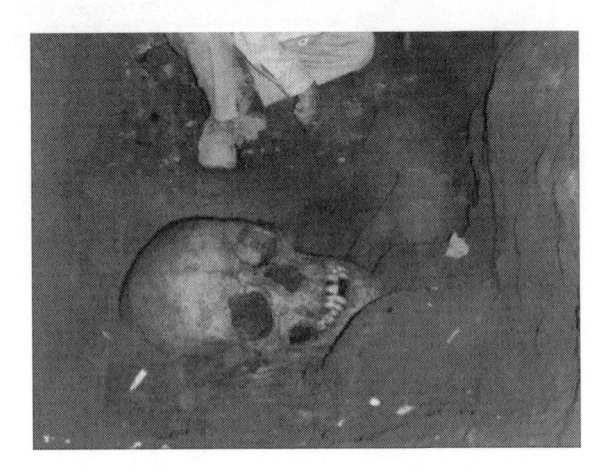

78

94. This Fake Isn't Even A Good One

95. One of The More Convincing Fakes At First Glance

100 Pics That Prove Nephilim Giants Existed

96. They Would Be More Focused On The Giant If It Were Real

97. Why Is Everyone Ignoring The Giant Human Skull?

98. Where's All of The Excavation Equipment?

100 Pics That Prove Nephilim Giants Existed

99. The Fakes Need To Be Exposed So The Evidence Can Prevail

100. This Fake Looks Fake and Thankfully Didn't Fool Anyone

The Breakdown

We've seen real archaeological evidence of giants and we've seen the fakes. No matter what position we take with the evidence, the fact remains that stories of giants have existed since early on in mankind's history. Skeptics would love for us to accept the explanation that most humans were just shorter in the past, but that doesn't account for the stories that contain exact measurements. At the end of the day, there is evidence that what we're being told to believe is not what matches the archaeological record, and that by itself should make us want to dig deeper for the truth.

Please Leave A Five Star Review

★★★★★

If you enjoyed reading this book, please leave a five star review on Amazon. Your review is important because it helps our people decide if they want to buy the book. If you believe what is written in this book is important, please take a few moments to leave a review. Thanks in advance.

Made in United States
Orlando, FL
12 November 2022